Still Life with Defeats
Naturaleza muerta con derrotas

Still Life with Defeats
Naturaleza muerta con derrotas

Tatiana Oroño

Translated by Jesse Lee Kercheval

WHITE PINE PRESS / BUFFALO, NEW YORK

White Pine Press
P.O. Box 236
Buffalo, NY 14201
www.whitepine.org

Publication of this book was supported by a grant from the National Endowment for the Arts, which believes that a great nation deserves great art; and by the Amazon Literary Partnership. We would also like to thank Lorin and Margorie Tiefenthaler and the Graduate School of the University of Wisconsin-Madison for their support.

Acknowledgments:
Atlanta Review: "es nuevamente el día" / "is newly the day,"
Drunken Boat: "Aviso" / "Warning," "[una vez]" / "[one time]," and "[en lugar de pelar la naranja]" / "[in place of peeling an orange]"
Guernica: "Náufragos" / "Shipwrecked"
International Poetry Review: "Estación Central" / "Central Station"
Ploughshares: "Aporía" / "Aporia," "Elogio del camino" / "Elegy of the Road, "Sin titulo" / "Untitled,"
Stand: "Tejidos" / "Lace," "Esto no es un sonajero" / "This Is Not a Baby Rattle," and "Descontados" / "Discounted"
Western Humanities Review: "Precisiones" / "Precision," "el habla desangrada" / "the bloodless speech" and "con qué hacíamos poesía" / "we made poetry with it"
World Literature Today: "Circe Maia" and "De pronto es el caballo" / "Suddenly There is the horse"

Printed and bound in the United States of America.

Cover image: "Muerte en la calle" by Dumas Oroño.

ISBN 978-1-945680-36-6

Library of Congress Control Number: 2019994707

Table of Contents

Introduction

Tatiana Oroño (San José, Uruguay, 1947) is the author of the poetry collections *Estuario* (2015), *La Piedra Nada Sabe* (2008), *Morada móvil* (2004), *Tajos* (1990), *Bajamar* (1996), *Cuenta abierta* (1986), *Poemas* (1982), *El alfabeto verde* (1979) and two bilingual Spanish/French editions of her work, *Tout fut ce qui ne fut pas / Todo tuvo la forma que no tuvo* (2004), translated by Laura Masello and *Ce qu'il faut dire a des fissures* (2012), translated by Madeleine Stratford; as well as the poetic memoir *Libro de horas* (2017). In 2009, Oroño won the Bartolomé Hidalgo Prize in Poetry and the Morosoli Prize for Poetry, two of the most important Uruguayan literary prizes. *Naturaleza muerta con derrotas / Still Life with Defeats: Selected Poems of Tatiana Oroño* is the first English-language collection of Oroño's poetry.

Tatiana Oroño is widely acknowledged as an essential voice in contemporary Uruguayan poetry. But that's too narrow a claim for her work. She is an essential poet. Period.

I first became aware of Tatiana Oroño's poetry when I was in Uruguay in 2014, looking for poets to include in *América invertida: An Anthology of Emerging Uruguayan Poets*. As I met with people, gathering suggestions for this anthology of poets under forty, her name kept coming up as someone—outside the anthology—that I just had to read. I was already translating poets who were over the age of forty, such as Idea Vilariño (1920 – 2009) and Circe Maia (1932), but I had not yet read Tatiana Oroño's work. On that trip, I was lucky

9

enough to meet Tatiana who arranged for me to receive a copy of her book *La piedra nada sabe*. I immediately fell in love with her inventive, experimental voice.

Since then, we have met often and I have translated her poetry, publishing it in magazines in the U.S. and U.K. such as *Ploughshares, Guerinca, World Literature Today, Stand* and the *Western Humanities Review*. We often meet in Montevideo at the cafe El Sportman across from the National Library, or for tea in her home in Malvin, a neighborhood of Montevideo long favored by writers and artists. I have been lucky enough to read her poems and poetic prose pieces ahead of their publication in her latest books, *Estuario* and *Libro del horas*, as well as her book-in-progress, *Neblina*, or—luckier still—to listen to her read them out loud to me. I have also heard her read her own work in public. In 2018, I attended a lovely reading and concert of her poems set to music by Daniel Petruchelli in the Museo Gurvich in Montevideo, an event that drew on the long tradition in Uruguay of poetry set to music or used as the lyrics in popular or political songs.

Hearing Tatiana Oroño's poetry in a museum seemed especially fitting. She is the daughter of the well-known Uruguayan artist, Dumas Oroño. She often writes about art in her reviews and essays and in her poetry. In this collection, her poems "Canto de Línea / Line's Edge" and "De pronto es el caballo / Suddenly there is the horse" touch on her father's work and "como una fruta seca / like a dried fruit" is another gorgeous ekphrastic poem. But in all her poetry she writes with a precise sensitivity, often using the white of the page as her canvas, making the space count as much as her exquisitely chosen words. In this, her work reminds me of Charles Olsen, Cole Swensen, or Carl Phillips, masters of spareness, white space, the line and the line break. She also is a master of the prose poem, drawing on the French tradition of Baudelaire, Rimbaud, Mallarmé and Ponge.

In all her forms, Oroño's subject matter is deeply felt, deeply personal to her, with poems about motherhood, the losses in the Uruguayan dictatorship of the 1980s and, most of all, the natural world. Indeed, a passionate environmentalist, Oroño finds her palate of images in nature. Her poems "El ginkgo / The ginkgo" and "quién le pone el silenciador a la moto? / who puts the muffler on the motorcycle?" remind me strongly of the ecopoetry of Juliana Spahr and Forrest Gander. She is also a feminist and her

10

poems show a consciousness of her own body, of being a woman in the pain and wonder of the everyday. But most of all, Oroño has a special awareness of language as a body of its own. Time and again she writes poems about poetry, poems that reclaim for poetry the power to give meaning to life.

I've purposefully used comparisons to poets well known to American poetry readers to locate Tatiana Oroño where she deserves to be, as a poet with a universal voice and message. It would be a mistake to see her as a poet to be read only by people with a special interest in poetry in translation, or poetry from Latin America, Her work deserves to reach a larger audience and this book is the big step in the process. This battle—to have work in translation reach a larger audience—is an ongoing one and one of my personal passions.

As a translator I am well aware that only approximately three percent of the books published in this country are works in translation. *Three Percent*, the translation website run by University of Rochester's translation program, goes further stating, "In terms of literary fiction and poetry, the number is actually closer to 0.7 percent." Of that 0.7 percent, the odds of being translated into English are even worse for female writers. In October, 2015, *Women in Translation* published an analysis of books published from 2010 to 2014 by thirty major publishers of translated works and found only twenty-four percent of the translated authors were women.

The situation is particularly pronounced in the case of Latin American women poets. Whenever I read an anthology of Latin American or South American poetry, even the most recent ones, I am always frustrated by the poor representation of women poets. In one recent anthology only three of eighteen "essential" poets were women. Uruguay, with only 3.3 million people, is the smallest Spanish-speaking country in South America, but it alone has produced more essential poets—who also happen to be women—than that. Uruguay has a long and strong tradition of women poets, starting with early poets such as Juana de Ibarbourou (1885–1979) and Delmira Agustini (1886–1914) and continuing through poets born in the 1920s such as Idea Vilariño, mentioned above, Amanda Berenguer, and Ida Vitale down through Marosa di Giorgio and Circe Maia, both a decade younger. Tatiana Oroño stands next in that lineage in time, but as a poetic equal. It is a tradition that continues to the present with the younger poets featured in *América invertida*

and to poets who, in their teens and twenties, are younger still.

I am often asked why there are so many women poets in Uruguay, what makes this tradition possible. To be honest, there is no perfect answer. Uruguayans often mention education as the reason. With the passing of the 1877 Law of Common Education, Uruguay pioneered universal, free and compulsory primary education in the Americas. There is a secular, national system with equal education for both sexes.

But, to me, the tradition exists, unbroken, for the slightly circular reason that each generation of women poets is aware of her predecessors, is aware of the possibility of becoming a poet because of the poets who came before her. I found Tatiana Oroño's poetry because young poets told me about her work. One of the first poets to mention her to me was the Uruguayan poet Virginia Lucas. Virginia and I went on to edit *Mis razones*, a collection of essays by Uruguayan women poets, nearly all about other Uruguayan women poets. The collection was published by the Nacional Library of Uruguay. Tatiana Oroño, who knows all the work of Uruguayan women poets, has one of her own essays in the collection about Amanda Berenguer. This tradition nourishes poetry in Uruguay, creating a poetry that I believe deserves to be better known and read in the rest of the world. And in *Still Life with Defeats*, Tatiana Oroño's poems are at last available in English, opening to a wider audience her vision of the beauty hidden in the natural world and in the language we humans share.

Still Life with Defeats
Naturaleza muerta con derrotas

Quiero escribir los versos

que se aten
a lo que conocí a las cosas que quise
versos restitutivos de los tiempos fueron
como animales mansos
masticando los pastos de mi primera vida.

Quiero escribir un verso en donde cante
mi ligadura al modo que viví
mi destino grupal.

(y que se escriba
con el corazón alto y un latido
perdiguero y delgado.)

I want to write the poems

that fit
with what I knew with the things I loved
restorative poems about the times that were
like tame animals
chewing the pastures of my first life.

I want to write a line where I sing
of my ties to the way I lived
my collective destiny.

(and that is written
with a high heart and a beat
gun dog and thin.)

Canto de Línea

para mi padre

Ahí estás. Cilíndrica
mente   blanco   hueco

diametralmente
                    abierto.

Eres un jarro puro.

Eres un jarro blanco
donde sube la leche

donde hierve y se encrespa
                            es un purísimo
foso
resbaloso
y calcáreo.

Donde se enrosca y calla
y persevera
y se enfría

(al baño de maria).

Line's Edge

for my father *(artist Dumas Oroño, 1921 – 2005)*

There you are. Cylindri-
cal   white   hollow

diametrically
            open.

You are a pure jug.

You are a white jug
where the milk rises

where it boils and curls
                        in a purism
pit
slippery
and calcareous.

Where it coils and silences
and perseveres
and cools

(in the bain-marie).

Purism is an art movement co-founded by the architect Le Corbusier. Fernand Léger was another key artist associated with purism. Purism aimed to give mechanical and industrial subject matter a timeless, classical quality.

Síntesis

La manzana sostiene
su copa cenital cruenta terráquea
en el éxtasis rojo
de la mañana

su inocente bocado de curva carne leve
en el vértice exacto
de la carne llagada

en abanico

en ascuas.

Synthesis

The apple holds up
its crowning cup terraqueous
bloody in the red ecstasy
of morning

innocent curved mouthful of flesh slight
at the exact apex
of the wound

a fan

in the embers.

Los polvos del día

Mi infancia tiene rotas
las losas del umbral

Las enfundadas salas aguardan
en espejos
evaporados lisos
de olvido y de metal

Suben
guías de hiedra
                tentaculares hojas sigilosas
por el hueso de piedra amurallada

y el tallo vegetal de mi niñez retoña
diminutos racimos de glicinas amargas

allí
                bajo los arcos
                                de la tarde baldía
en un jardín claustral
va la memoria
con sus frágiles hebras remecidas

allí
en la poniente
gloria
de los polvos del día, mi infancia

sobre el lienzo
de las tardes
bordaba
con hilos vespertinos
los primeros fantasmas

Day's Dust

My childhood has broken
stones on the threshold

The shrouded rooms wait
in mirrors
smooth evaporating
forgetfulness and metal

Ivy
rises
            stealthy leaves tentacles
through the bone of walled stone

and the stem of my childhood sprouts
tiny clusters of bitter wisteria

there
            under the arches
                        of the idle afternoon
in a cloistered garden
memory moves
with its fragile waving strands

there
in setting
glory
of the day's dust, my childhood

on the canvas
of late afternoons
the first ghosts
embroidered
with threads of evening

Lo que vive

Toco tu mano hijo
y desde el piso se alza

el cuerno de la muerte

embravecido
embiste
asesta
cela

la carne
acurrucada

estoy temblando.

What is Alive

I touch your hand son
and from the floor rises

the horn of death

enraged
it attacks
charges
guarding

your flesh curled,
nestled

I am shaking.

Descontados

Aquí ha pasado algo

Hasta hace poco éramos
sol y sal de la tierra

Homosapiens. Max Scheler.

Ahora somos esto:
los que estamos

afuera de la cuenta

de 90 000 muertos o desaparecidos

> los ojos.
> los oídos.
> tentativos.

Discounted

Here, something has happened

Until recently, we were
sun and salt of the earth

Homo sapiens. Max Scheler.

Now we are this:
those that are

outside the count

of 90, 000 dead or disappeared

        the eyes.
        the ears.
        wary.

De pronto es el caballo
(en el mate) el perfil
                    delicado

masticando

de pronto es eso solo
—es eso solo—
lo que me salva
                              —ese dibujo—el trazo calcinado
                                            del caballo
esa cabeza equina que claudica en la línea
                              el dorso
del caballo
la cabeza
instintiva
              que triangula equidista la memoria
aboceta
la cintura rumiante

en el diafragma
frágil   la calabaza
seca.

Suddenly there is the horse
(on the maté gourd) the profile
                    delicate

chewing

suddenly it is that alone
—is that alone—
that saves me

                              —this drawing—charcoal trace
                                        of the horse
this equine head that rests on the line
                              the back
of the horse
the head
instinctive
                    that triangulates the equidistant memory
sketches
the ruminate waist

in the diaphragm
the gourd   fragile
dry.

                    (after an etching on a gourd by Dumas Oroño)

Poética

poesía es
cuando no le hago sombra
cuando filtra

porosa
persuadida

no yo, este comportamiento

esta manera dada sostenida
                    adentro/afuera

Poetics

poetry is
when I do not overshadow it
when it filters

porous
persuasive

not me, this behavior

this way it is given, sustained
                    inside/outside

Tarea en entredicho

Dar cuenta involucrar
los hechos probarles
la existencia
de palabra

por fuerza
casi
nada:

veinte años atrás
        todo tuvo la forma
                que no tuvo

salpicada
mordida

de una orilla.

Task in Question

To give an account involving
the facts, to prove
their existence
by the word

inevitably
almost
nothing:

twenty years ago
                everything was all
                        it was not

bursting
bite

of a river bank

Precisiones

Preciso es elegir qué deberá salvarse. Elegir qué nos salva.

Esta tierra debajo huele a verano a flora abigarrada.

Es una antigua tumba de hojas mordidas.
De bocas y de manos. Poblada tumba
humana donde ha sido flechada
de sed de vivir
con un ínfimo
dardo:

una pluma de ánade
        una pluma raspante
                una tecla en el blanco.

Precisions

Choose, with precision, what must be saved. Choose what saves us.

This land below smells of summer, of variegated flora.

It is an ancient tomb of chewed leaves.
Of mouths and hands. Crowded human
tomb that has been shot through
by the thirst for life
with a very small
dart:

a duck feather
      a rough feather
            a hit dead on the target.

Frutalidad

Soy un durazno : hollejo
                y pulpa.

Y el corazón, de pómez.

En la carne amarilla surca lo cotidiano. Monda muerde
hinca el diente.

                No sé
                dentro el hueso
                de la pepita tierna qué quién
late a la médula.

Coraza del carozo cierra el paso.

Fruitility

I am a peach : skin
         and pulp.

And the heart, pumice-stone.

The everyday cuts through the yellow flesh. The tooth thrusts
bites through the peel.

         I do not know
         inside the bone
         of the tender pip what who
beats at the heart.

The shield of the stone seals the way.

Náufragos

El Náufrago encontró

papel botella
tizón o estilográfica
para garabatear *socorro estoy aquí*

y fue izado a cubierta con su heredad
de huesos arriado en la litera
y los ojos cerró como un enfermo en cama y se dejó llevar
como un gurí.

Le dijeron *asímejorasí* en las plantas la piel
le dijeron *sísí*
volvé
las manos que estiraron las sábanas.

Ese volvió.

El nadar de océano
gemelo al casco al costillar del barco
le instruyó al corazón cómo bracear cómo
sobrevivir le dijeron las manos desde aquí y el palmoteo
del mar del otro lado.

A ese
lo envolvió el cuchicheo de las mesas servidas.
Se lo tragó la tribu.

Pero qué fue
lo último
que oyeron
todos los que no hallaron ni pluma ni carbón

Shipwrecked

The Castaway found

paper bottle
half-burnt stick or pen
to scribble *help I am here*

and he was hoisted on the deck with his inheritance
of bones lowered in the berth
and his eyes closed like a patient in a sick bed and he was carried along
like a boy.

They told him *likethis* better *likethis* on the soles the skin
the hands that stretched the sheets
said to him *yesyes*
come back to us!

He came back.

The ocean swimming
twin to the hull to the boat's ribs
He taught his heart how to swim how
to survive his hands told him go from here to there
as the sea applauded on the other side.

For this
he was folded into the whisper of the linen dining tables.
The tribe swallowed him up.

But that was
the last
that they heard
of all those who found neither pen nor charcoal

ni botella
ni vos

porque sólo había arena alrededor.

nor bottle
nor you

because there was only sand all around.

Lo que hay es lo que falta

No puedo contar porque lo que tengo que contar no está, no se produjo. Es lo que se produce cuando escribo.

Mejor dicho: hay una historia. La de las sombras de la mano, la del calor que desprendió la mano al moverse buscando. Es una historia fuera de los hechos contados que—como la sombra—está fuera de los cuerpos.

Mi empeño es encontrarla. La historia es ésa.

What is There is Missing

I can't tell you because what I have to tell is not there; it didn't happen. It's what happens when I write.

Or better to say: there is a story. One about the shadows of the hand, the heat released when the hand is moving, searching. It is a story outside the facts—like the shadow—is outside the body.

My task is to find it. That is story.

Construir

en el polvo
cimentar en la lava
excavar en el aire
apuntalar en punto imaginario

sostener la mirada

contener el aliento

levantar el andamio.

To Build

in the dust
to cement in the lava
to dig in the air
to prop up in imaginary spot

to hold the gaze

to hold your breath

to raise the scaffold.

Química

La del químico es una curiosidad aliada a la sospecha y una forma disimulada de la transgresión: es posible desenmascarar esto al mezclarlo con aquello otro. Una cadena libre muestra cosas que la sustancia mantenía ocultas. Quien se comporte como un químico, pero fuera de laboratorio, será perseguido.

Chemistry

The chemist's is a curiosity allied with suspicion and a disguised form of disobedience: it is possible to unmask this by mixing it with another. An open chain shows what the substance kept secret. Whoever behaves like a chemist, but outside the laboratory, will be persecuted.

Nada de palabras

Él le pidió que fuera a buscar algo cualquiera en el bolsillo del saco y ella encontró la carta. Camas y platos no se movieron. Contando a la niña los tres siguieron viviendo en el mismo lugar. La desdicha dio a luz una mujer torpe. La mujer del amante de la otra mujer. Amante es una palabra que encierra el pecho y los riñones. Él se volvió también el instructor de una lógica codificadora de los derechos positivos del adulterio: se repudia a la mujer porque no se la desea se la repudia porque es torpe y no entiende los hechos. Dado que no entiende se la repudia cada día y cada noche para mejor persuadirla. Nada de palabras. Nada de miradas. Se evitará el mínimo roce a fin de que su alma se desgaste. Toda palabra quedará fuera del hostigamiento del repudio ocioso. Silenciosas maniobras cotidianas de usurpación conyugal consumadas por el hombre tejen la abdicación de ella. El derecho de traición el derecho de mutismo son aprobados por el ciclo ininterrumpido de rutinas. Mantenerlas disminuye los márgenes de riesgo del vencedor al tiempo que arruina y extenúa a la vencida. Es necesario dañarla. Desarraigar su amor empecinado. Ni una sola palabra dará agua a esos sentimientos sedientos. No habrá nada que decir. El silencio apuntará directamente al corazón amortajado de la mujer que se calla.

No words

He asked her to look for something in his jacket pocket and she found the letter. The beds and plates did not tremble. Counting the little girl, all three continued living in the same place. Misfortune gave birth to a foolish woman. Wife of the lover of another woman. Lover is a word that cages the chest and kidneys like animals. He also became her instructor in the logic codifying the rules of adultery: the woman is disowned because she is unwanted, is foolish because she doesn't understand the facts. Since she doesn't understand, she is disowned every day and every night to persuade her. Not a word. Not a glance. The slightest touch is avoided so her soul is worn down. Every word is left outside in the harassment of the condemned useless woman. Silent daily maneuvers of complete conjugal usurpation consummated by the man hatching his renunciation of her. The uninterrupted cycle of routine reinforces the right of treason the right of silence. Maintaining them lowers the margin of risk for the winner while destroying and exhausting the loser. It is necessary to wound her. To root out her stubborn love. Not a single word to water those thirsty feelings. There will be nothing to say. Silence aimed at the shrouded heart of the woman who is silenced.

Mi madre

acreería creerá me cree.
Voy hacia ese acrecer ese creer.

Caer en ese cántaro. Decaer en el pie de esa fe.

De ese mirar.

Mi madre mira. Abre camino.
Camino hasta el mirar. Voy hacia él. Le creo

lo que brilla
en el ojo.
Tras él. Tras él le creo.

Lo que no se le ve.

My mother

would believe she'll believe she believes me.
I'm going towards that belief.

To fall in that jug. To decay at the foot of that faith.

Of that glance.

My mother looks. She opens the way.
I walk toward the glance. I go to him. I believe him

what shines
in his eye.
Through him. Through him I believe him.
What you can not see.

El deseo

Todo tuvo la forma
que no tuvo. Pero tiene

el deseo

persistencia una forma fluida un amarre
de aguas. Más
del 50% de los cuerpos
es agua tornasol del abrazo
molecular de hache
en torno a O.

En la suerte corrida en lo vivido
en su fe de bitácora cuenta

ese suelo lacustre esa morada móvil esa frontera líquida

su espermático
don de dividirse

en flujos en
regatos en subsuelos
barrosos. Mi mano palma y dorso
también es agua orilla burilada
por el deseo
que siempre borra el trazo.

Tanta agua humedece la historia.
Hace duda su suerte. Húmeda.

Desire

Everything took the shape
it did not have. But

desire

persists a fluid form a berth
for water. More than
50% of the body
is water sheen of the molecular
embrace of H
around O.

Water counts on a lucky life
on its faith in the ship's log

that lake floor that moving abode that liquid frontier

its spermatic
gift of dividing itself

in streams in
pools in muddy
subsoils. My palm, the back of my hand,
are also shorelines inscribed
by the desire
that erases all traces.

So much water moistens the story.
Doubts its luck. Wet as a tongue.

La piedra nada sabe

La piedra nada sabe
bruñida por la lluvia en esta hora.
Carbónica.
Mojada.

Nada sabe del viaje. Aquí apuntala
cuando el sol austral muerde el aire
                macizos de amarilis.
          Flores rojas
que aguantan lluvias
viento bajo la piel de ozono
quebradiza
el sol ácido/ a pesar de ese nombre
botánico
rozado por estambres y pistilos con mano amable
tersa
de musa gongorina
pastoril/ de hojas como espadas mi macizo de flores.
                          Que la piedra apuntala.

        Nada sabe la piedra
        que recogí en Malvín
                la playa

        donde el padre, Gerardo jugaba
        con Daniel.

        La piedra estaba allí

The Stone Knows Nothing

The stone knows nothing
burnished by the rain now.
Carbonic.
Wet.

It knows nothing of the trip. Here, when the winter sun
bites the air, it props up

                     a clump of amaryllis
                     Red flowers
that withstand rain
wind beneath the skin of ozone
sickly
acid sun / in spite of that name
a botanist
brushed the stamens and pistils with a friendly hand
smooth
as the pastoral muse
of Góngora/ with leaves like swords my mound of flowers.

                                   The stone supports them.

          The stone does not know
          I picked it up in Malvin
                 the beach

          where the father, Gerardo played
          with Daniel.

The stone was there.

Elogio del camino

Pregunto adónde van las cosas que no llegaron a destino. La mayoría de las cosas. El inventario mayor del mundo. Adónde van a parar las cosas que no van a parar a ningún lado. Las que se malogran, las que no tienen remedio. Pregunto adónde van.

La poesía es el lugar adonde van las cosas que no tienen solución. A buscarla.

Elegy for the Road

Where do they go, I ask, the things that never arrived at their destination. Most things. The largest inventory in the world. Where do they end up, the things that do not end up anywhere. Those that fail, those that have no remedy. I ask where do they go.

Poetry is the place where the things go that have no solution. To look for it.

Aporía

Océano no hay
sin naufragios ni ahogados
sin víctimas
no hay

      océano
que no lama una orilla

      como a llaga
      o herida.

Aporia

Ocean, there is none
without shipwrecks, without the drowned
without victims
there is no

      ocean
that does not lick the shore

      like a sore
      or a wound.

Tejidos

Alguien me enseñó a tejer con bolillos y aprendí. En un patio con glorieta, fuente de azulejos moriscos y tuberías rotas. La labor consistía en ir siguiendo el dibujo del modelo en papel pinchado sobre un almohadilla alargada con varios hilos en cuyas puntas, atados, los bolillos sonaban, al chocar entre sí, con minúsculo zapateo. La almohadilla estaba acostada sobre una especie de cama de muñecas. No era una cama, se llamaba escalerilla. Con ella en la falda aprendí a pasar de un lado a otro los trémulos garrotes que al irse entrecruzando iban trabando un tejido arborescente. Mi instructora lo remató. La labor calada sin gancho de aguja era fruto de un juego al aire libre, resultado de un baile de pequeños zuecos de boj.

Lace

Someone taught me to make lace with bobbins and I learned. In a courtyard with a gazebo, fountain of Moorish tiles and broken pipes. The task consisted of following the paper pattern pinned over an elongated pillow with various threads on whose ends, tied, the bobbins sounded, when they struck each other, like tiny shoes tapping. The pillow was resting on sort of a doll's bed. It was not a bed--it was called a box. With it in my lap, I learned how to pass from one side to another the tremulous rods that, crisscrossing, weaved together intricate lace tree. My teacher finished it off. The pierced work without crochet hook was the fruit of a outdoor game, the result of a dance of tiny boxwood clogs.

Sin título

Quedaba un cielo azul
Y todo lo demás

No

Untitled

A blue sky remained
Everything else

No

Estación Central

Cuando íbamos a viajar, una vez por año, el día empezaba de noche. Madrugábamos y las cosas entraban a los ojos más llenas de luz. De una luz más levantada y potente, con refracciones que inundaban el comedor y se multiplicaban en los rincones iluminados a deshora. En las tazas del desayuno apurado bajo luz artificial rebotaba el chorro de agua. Anómalo. Subíamos con los sentidos encandilados en el taxi a oscuras. Nos dejaba en la Estación Central. Por cualquier entrada se desembocaba en el hall que atravesábamos como si supiéramos que el cielo sólo aclararía después de haber subido en penumbras al vagón. Y sólo amanecería, con olor a tierra, cuando el tren partiera. Mientras tanto el cielo esperaría. Caminábamos en dirección a la boletería como si nos reabsorbiera la inmovilidad del sueño. La extensión nos bebía los pasos. El vendedor daba pasajes recortado en la ventanilla de barrotes de bronce siempre lejana. Caminábamos en el tumulto de los viajeros sumergidos en el tamaño inabarcable del viaje.

Central Station

When we went traveling, once a year, the day started at night. We got up early and things more full of light entered our eyes. Of a light more elevated and potent, with reflections that flooded the dining room and multiplied in the illuminated corners at an inconvenient time. In the cups of the hurried breakfast the water from the faucet changed color under artificial light. An anomaly. With senses dazzled, we got into the cab in the dark. It let us off at the Central Station. Every entry flowed into the hall that we crossed as if we knew the sky would only lighten after we had gotten into the train in the penumbra. And only would dawn, with a smell of earth, when the train left. Meanwhile the sky would wait. We walked toward the ticket office as if re-absorbed by the immobility of sleep. The distance drank our steps. The agent who sold tickets was silhouetted in the window with bars of bronze always distant. We walked in the tumult of the travelers submerged in the unfathomable size of the journey.

Esto no es un sonajero ·

Un ruido como de cristalitos.
Cositas que se rompen.
Un ruido de filosos
pedacitos.

Un ruidito en el piso del alma
traquetea. Un tuerquita
floja.

Quién se agacha y tantea
en los filitos. Quién
se arrodilla y palpa
en los crics. En las señitas sueltas.

This Is Not A Baby Rattle

A noise like tiny crystals.
Tiny things that break.
A noise of sharp
tiny pieces.

A tiny noise on the floor of the soul
clatters. A tiny loose
screw.

One stoops and feels
for the tiny shards. One
kneels and feels
the tiny crunching. In the tiny
scattered signs.

Aviso

Hay un hueco en el cuerpo de la mujer a la altura de la cincha del tórax, del abdomen. Se tira de la cama a las cuatro de la mañana porque la noche le da aviso. El hueco no duerme. ¿Cómo va a dormir un hueco?, si falta.

Eso avisa la noche. Como una madre.

Warning

There is a hole in the woman's body at the height of a girth strap, of the abdomen. She throws herself from the bed at four o'clock in the morning because the night gave her a warning. The hole does not sleep. How can a hole go to sleep? if it's not there.

The night gave that warning. Like a mother.

Huecos

El ombú tenía un hueco del tamaño de una cueva entre los troncos que se le retorcían alrededor, enrocados a la mismo raíz gesticulante como un montón de manos con tendones y nudillos como piedra. El hueco era el lugar del primer trunco del que ya no quedaban ni las cortezas. Me asomé.

El ombú es el único árbol que no muere nunca, dijo. Cuando se seca le crecen otros troncos.

Después nos sentamos en unos bancos. Cuando se hizo de noche apagaron el fuego y nos mandaron a dormir.

Yo soñé que estaba en una reunión donde la gente hablaba de cosas distintas. Un hombre decía que estábamos en la esclavitud porque la semana pasada en Florida un camión llevó a dos hermanos junto con la motosierra a un monte, les dejó la comida del día y no volvió más, estuvieran seis días talando sin comer y a uno le cayó por encima un tronco que el otro serruchó para poder sacarlo, y después que lo sacó se fue corriendo tres kilómetros a avisar y volvió corriendo pero la ambulancia, cuatro horas después, ya no tuvo nada que hacerle. La mujer de mechitas le decía a la otra que el labial era cremoso y que ella no dejaba al marido solo un fin de semana con auto y plata en el bolsillo, ni loca. La otra se reía y el hombre le decía a la periodista que estaba tomando whisky con coca que ni una palabra de lo que acababa de oír. Porque además, desde que controlan las empresas de construcción hay muchos menos accidentes: un solo muerto en lo que va del año, decía, pero como a las rurales no los controla a nadie porque pase lo que pase nadie se entera, le decía el hombre al vaso. Y me di cuenta de que ella, allá abajo del maquillaje, no había podido escuchar nada, Y me di vuelta en la cama para seguir durmiendo. Soñé que me caía adentro del ombú.

Holes

The ombú had a hole the size of a cave between the trunks which twisted around it, each grounded in the same root, gesticulating like countless hands with tendons and knuckles like stone. The hole was where the first trunk had been but now there nothing, not even bark. I peered in.

The ombú is the only tree that never dies, it's said, When one trunk dries up, others grow.

Later we sat on one of the benches. When night came, we put the fire out and went off to sleep.

I dreamed I was at a meeting where people talked about different things. A man said we were living in slavery because last week in Florida a truck took two brothers with a chainsaw to a eucalyptus grove, left them with food for a day, and never came back. They spent six days logging without food and one had a trunk fall on him that the other sawed until he could get it off and after he did, he ran three kilometers to let someone know and returned running but when the ambulance arrived four hours later, there nothing to be done. The woman with highlights told the other woman that the lipstick was creamy, and that she was not leaving her husband alone for the weekend with a car and money in his wallet; she was not crazy. The woman reporter laughed and the man told her that he was drinking whiskey with coke and had not heard a word that. Because, besides, now they were regulating the construction industry, there were fewer accidents; a single death so far this year, he said, but in the country no one regulates any one because no matter what happens, nobody finds out, the man said to his glass. And I realized the woman, there underneath her make-up, hadn't been able to hear anything. I turned over in bed to stay asleep. And I dreamed I fell inside the ombú.

Preguntas con filo

Te preguntas qué es bueno.
Cuál el punzón, la punta del compás.
Tiendes la mano a la idea de concentración.
Tiendes a comprender
que concentrar
es ser. Que ser
es lo que quieres.

Que querer ser es bueno.

Comprendes que concentrar es desechar.

Estás dispuesta.
Afilas tus navajas.

Questions with an Edge

You wonder what's good.
Where's the awl, the point of the compass.
You stretch a hand toward the idea of concentration.
You stretch to understand
that to concentrate
is to be. That being
is what you want.

That wanting to be is good.

You understand that to concentrate is to discard.

You are willing.
You sharpen your knives.

Ganar el pan

Ganar el pan de la poesía significa primero entender lenguas. Segundo, hablar alguna o varias. Chapucearlas al menos. Cómo se dice esto en esta. Así. Y esto en aquella: ¿así o así? A ver, fíjate cómo dice la gente, qué no dice, cómo se calla. Por qué no dice. Porque hay cosas que no se dicen. ¿Por qué?

Ganar el pan con la poesía significa otra cosa. Quiere decir que la poesía se vendió. Con aquellos denarios o dineros se come sin necesidad de otras industrias. Hubo mercaderes que la compraron, ¿para ellos o para su señor? Quién lo sabe. Quizá esos mercaderes entiendan lenguas y busquen el pan de la poesía. Allá ellos, vos vas a comer. Pero seguirás viviendo en la plaza.

Ganar el pan de la poesía significa en segundo lugar vivir con el hatillo al hombro. No se conoce lenguas por pararse en la misma esquina o sentarse en el cordón de la vereda. Aunque se esté al desnudo. Hay que conocer los sinsabores del vagabundeo para gustar el sabor del pan de las lenguas.

Ganar el pan con la poesía también quiere decir que tu vida por un lado se complicó. Tendrás que decidir si, con vivir en la plaza entre las voces del ir y venir del mercado, es suficiente. O habrás de echarte otra vez a los caminos aunque se haga el silencio completo. Hasta el tintineo del bolsillo enmudecerá.

El pan el pan. Nadie hace pan para comérselo solo. No es lo mismo que hacer un churrasco. La poesía. Eres tú. La lengua que te ve. El ojo que te dirige la palabra.

To Earn Your Daily Bread

To earn you daily bread with poetry means first to grasp languages. Second, to speak one or more. At least to gossip in them. Know how to say this in that one. Like this. And this in that one: like this or like that? To see, to notice how people speak, what they don't say, when they shut up. Why they don't speak. Because there are things they don't say. Why?

To earn you daily bread with poetry means another thing. It means that the poetry sold. With those denarii or denarius you can eat without the need of other work. There were merchants who bought it. For themselves or for their master? Who knows. Perhaps those merchants understand languages, are in pursuit of the bread of poetry. Because of that, you are going to eat. But still you live on the street.

To earn you daily bread with poetry also means living with hobo's bindle on your shoulder. You do not learn languages by standing on the same corner or sitting on the curb. Not even naked. You have to know the worries of wandering to taste the taste of the bread of tongues.

To earn you daily bread with poetry means that your life in some ways will be complicated. You will have to decide if living on the street among the voices of coming and going from the market is enough. Or if you will have resume your journey until absolute silence falls and everything goes silent, even the jingling in your pocket.

The bread the bread. Nobody makes bread to eat it alone. It is not the same as grilling a steak. The poetry. It's you. The language that sees you. The eye that speaks to you.

Encaje de Brujas

En mi familia éramos laicos, gente sin fiestas de comunión ni bautismos, ni esa ilusión de vestidos blancos que compartían los demás. Pero a los 7 años sentí el llamado de la fe. Con la punta de los dedos eché mano a un panadero a la deriva. Porque sabía que si arrancaba la semilla, un pan diminuto invaginado en el pompón ingrávido, podría pedir un deseo. Pedí que mi padre volviera y riera ella, porque una madre sin risa es algo complicado. Lo dejé en el aire y ahí quedó, en suspenso, indeciso. Soplé para que se llevara el pedido a destino. Que no podía ser otro que la buena voluntad de Dios. Quien tenía que estar de mi parte.

Años después escribí un nombre de varón en un vidrio empañado. El vidrio era casi tan alto y ancho como la pared. Afuera, de noche. En la superficie condensada de frío desnudé letras que desquitaban del impredecible futuro calando en el cielo la escritura bordada por la punta del dedo. Estoy segura que los poderes puestos en obra por aquel conjuro eran de naturaleza inviolable. Puse al cielo en función indeleble de papel de calco. Así se golpea, comprendí, a las puertas del corazón de la misericordia. Desde adentro de esta casa triste y con un solo dedo grabar un nombre en la memoria del cielo es caer de rodillas sin doblarlas.

Años después el hijo la llamaba por teléfono desde el exilio en México. Ella me dijo por qué mantenía durante todos esos años el jardín con tanta pulcritud de podas, injertos y trasplantes, el año entero con la espalda doblada. Cuando me confió que trabajaba para que el día que él llegase lo encontrara todo lindo, como siempre, entendí.

También actúo así. Parecido. No vendrá nadie en Navidad. Pero estrené el mantel amarillo. Tapé el pan dulce con la servilleta bordada en España. Tampoco fue usada nunca. Dos piezas labradas con el arte del encaje de Brujas.

También actúo así. Parecido. No vendrá nadie en Navidad. Pero estrené el mantel amarillo. Tapé el pan dulce con la servilleta bordada en España. Tampoco fue usada nunca.

Dos piezas labradas con el arte del encaje de Brujas.

Lace from Bruges

In my family we were not religious, were people without celebrations of communion or baptism, or the illusion of white dresses others shared. But at 7, I felt the call of faith. With the tips of my fingers I pulled a dandelion apart. Because I knew if I could pluck out one seed, the tiny bead enfolded in the weightless pompon, I could make a wish. I asked for my father to come back and make my mother laugh, because a mother without laughter is complicated. I let the seed loose in the air and there it floated, in suspense, undecided. I blew so it would take my wish to its destination. Which could be none other than God's good will. God who had to be on my side.

Years later I wrote a man's name on fogged glass. The window was almost as tall and wide as the wall. Outside, night. In the cold condensation of the surface, I wrote naked letters to make up for the unpredictable future, casting in the sky the writing embroidered by the tip of my finger. I am sure the powers put into work by that spell were inviolable in nature. I put the sky in the indelible role of tracing paper. This is how you knock, I understood, at the doors of the heart of mercy. From inside this sad house and with only one finger to record a name in the memory of the sky is to fall on your knees without bending them.

Years later, her son called her by phone from exile in Mexico. She told me why she kept the garden with such neat pruning, grafting and transplantation during all those years, the whole year with her back bent. When she confided to me that she worked so that the day he arrived he would find everything beautiful, as always, I understood.

I also act like this. The same. No one will come at Christmas. But I opened the yellow tablecloth for the first time. I covered the sweet bread with the napkin embroidered in Spain. It has never been used before either. Two pieces trimmed with the art of Bruges lace.

I act like that too. The same. Nobody will come for Christmas. But I will open the yellow tablecloth for the first time. I cover the sweet bread with the napkin embroidered in Spain. It was never used before either.

Two pieces of cloth trimmed with the art of Bruges lace.

Pájaros

Un pájaro canta y otro otros. Laten, brotan. Corales. Son instrumentos de viento. Unos pulmoncitos que no pesan llenan la bóveda del canto. Puntas de aguja que bordan sonidos traslúcidos como el cielo. Un follaje de sonido único. En la horqueta de un trino viene a posarse otro y ya vuela otro, y así. Cuando llega el alba el canto de los pájaros es un cielo estrellado que ven los oídos.

Birds

A bird sings and another others. They throb, well up. Choirs. They are wind instruments. Tiny lungs that weigh nothing fill the vault of their song. Needle points embroidering translucent sounds like the sky. They pluck the air, treble and bass. Aerial. A foliage of singular sound. One comes to rest on the fork of a trill, another flies off, and so on. At dawn the song of the birds is a starry sky the ears see.

Quehaceres

Hice fuego. Levanté las paredes
y las bocas los fémures las filas de incisivos

y volví a los oficios de la caza.

Devueltos a las manos los oficios
de aljaba y puntería / oficios de pedrada
      de trampa
      bajo el suelo de hojas

juegan con los dos ojos / con las diez uñas diestras

     en desnucar la víctima.

Housework

I lit a fire. Raised the walls
and the mouths femurs rows of incisors

and went back to the trade of hunting.

My hands recovered the art
of the quiver and aim / of sling shot
            of trap
            under the carpet of leaves

they play with two eyes / with ten clever nails

            to break the neck of their victim.

en lugar de pelar la naranja
escribir el poema:

    pelaje
    que le quito
    sin estragos
    limpito

a la hora que vivo.

(memoria de salvador puig)

instead of peeling an orange
writing a poem:

pelt
I peel off
without wrecking havoc
cleanly

now I am alive.

la poesía no ocasiona daños colaterales
no derrama petróleo
no genera deuda pública
no establece bases militares
no levanta alambradas
no divide países
no abre fosas comunes
no disemina minas personales
no expulsa población civil
no genera campos de refugiados

                                        la poesía no daña
la poesía no daña

                la poesía no daña

                predispone
                a la palabra.

poetry does not cause collateral damage
does not spill oil
does not generate public debt
does not establish military bases
does not lay barbed wire
does not divide countries
does not open mass graves
does not spread land mines
does not expel civilian populations
does not generate refugee camps

                     poetry does no harm
poetry does no harm

       poetry does no harm

       it is predisposed
       to the word

con qué hacíamos poesía

juan carlos macedo y los demás
—nosotros—

(cuando todo caía
nosotros escribíamos)

peregrinos sin tierra prometida
hacíamos poesía

con poesía.

we made poetry with it

juan carlos macedo and others
—us—

(when everything fell
we wrote)

pilgrims without a promised land
we made poetry

with poetry.

es nuevamente el día y su invariable voluntad
de encender las cosas que dormitan / esa forma intrusiva
de intervenir torcer
el curso
del trabajo de ver
sin lentes
y sin luz.

it is day again and its invariable willingness
of igniting the things that slumber / this intrusive way
of intervening twisting
the course
of the work of seeing
without glasses
and without light.

otra vez mediodía se empecina en rodearte hacerte un cerco
de luz estrepitosa insidiosa
que aplana y atropella

      opaca quieta inmersa vos

      sin más asunto
      que estar a contramano de espaldas

      al sol

en el cenit.

again noon insists on surrounding you making a fence
of insidious boisterous light
that rolls and runs over you

        opaque calm immerses you

        with no more ado
        than walking backwards

        into the sun

at its zenith.

el mito de la estabilidad está bien como lo que es:
un consuelo contra la realidad.

the myth of stability is fine as what it is:
a consolation against reality.

una vez le pregunté a mi madre si ella hablaba con mi padre, si le hablaba de las cosas que sentía. no me contestó enseguida, estaba en un predio de silencio alambrado, le costaba moverse dentro de él. cercada en aquella quietud masticaba galleta. después se acercó hasta los labios y los movió: "a veces nos escribíamos."

once I asked my mother if she talked to my father, if she spoke to him of the things she felt. she did not answer me immediately, there was an acre of barbed-wire silence, it hard for her to move within it. fenced in the stillness she chewed a cracker. when the answer came close to her lips, it moved them: "sometimes we wrote to each other."

tatiana, ¿se abrió la puerta, entonces? ¿el sol entró
a la casa, trastabilló en los marcos, encandiló los ojos?
¿dos muchachas pisando con imperio

el sol suelo fragante? ¿te alzaron y ciñeron pulsera?

a ver, niña, dos reinas te sonríen
                    en san josé de mayo a tus tres años

vienen a ti no es mirra no es incienso es oro
aro redondo
tu puño es coronado.

tatiana, did the door open, then? the sun entered
the house. staggered across the threshold, dazzled the eyes?
two girls entered, stepping imperiously

on the sun fragrant ground? did they lift you and fasten the bracelet?

look, girl, two queens are smiling at you
                            in san josé de mayo at your three years

come to visit you it is not myrrh not incense it is gold
round hoop
your fist is crowned.

El ginkgo (que nos sobrevivirá) echó
sus hojas
despereza el follaje
arropa su crecer
erguido el pie ha expandido los brazos

son asuntos del patio: "áreas verdes "
no juega en esta cancha (no hay quien
se ponga
la vieja camiseta de los emprendimientos forestales:
ni a buschental ni a tomkinson ni a piria ni a lussich
les queda un hincha) la ley de la ciudad la del país
es otra: el árbol es negocio
                si se tala. Qué más da que dé sombra
no es commodity el fresco que arroje cada copa
aquí juega setiembre/octubre/tierra
negra/restos de té yerba café
aquí suena la savia que en los labios
de cada hoja que aflora que rebrota
a pesar de que los rayos uv
arrasen
        en campito vereda y cancha grande.

The ginkgo (which will outlive us) casts
its leaves
stretches its foliage
protecting its growth
stands upright spreading its arms

these are affairs of the courtyard: "green spaces"
do not play on this field (there is no one
to put on
the old team jersey of the forestation campaign
(not Buschental nor Tomkinson nor Piria nor Lussich
have a single fan left) the law of the city is one thing that of the country
is another: the tree is a business
                if it is felled. What does it matter that it gives shade?
the coolness the crown casts is not a commodity.
             here plays september/october /black
earth/ remains of tea yerba coffee
here plays the sap that sounds on the lips
of each leaf that emerges that rebounds
in spite of the UV rays
that sweep
              over sand lots and grand ball fields alike.

quién le pone el silenciador a la moto?
quién controla a la empresa tercerizada?
y a sus cuadrillas que hacen sebo una hora
a la sombra de única árbol
sin apagar los motores?
quién paga el combustible de la pala mecánica
prendida porque sí?
quién le para el carro al tipo
que decide no ir "pa'trás de cante
por agazzi / oncativo"? ("allá no es
una papa como aquí")
y a los otras cuadrillas y los capataces de los otras cuadrillas?
quién los hace cumplir?
quién le revisa los libros contables a las iglesias
multimillonarias
          exoneradas de impuestos?
quién me explica por qué
este año
no habrá reforestación en montevideo?
quién autoriza a los terratenientes a no pagar el impuesto
a la escuela pública?
quién le da pan al que no tiene dientes?

quién provee de ak47 (m1, ar15) al traficante
(amigo del juez)
          armado hasta los dientes?

who puts the muffler on the motorcycle?
who controls the subcontractors?
and their crews that chew the fat for an hour
in the shade of the only tree
without turning off their engines?
who pays for the fuel of the mechanical shovel
left on because why not?
who stops the truck, a guy
who decides not to go "back to the slum
by agazzi and oncativo streets"? ("over there
is not child's play like here")
and what about the other crews and crew's foremen?
who makes them comply?
who fixes the ledgers of the multi-millionaire
tax-except
                churches
who can explain to me why
this year
no trees were planted in montevideo?
who authorized the landowners not to pay
schools taxes?
who gives hard bread to those who have no teeth?

who provided the AK 47 (M1, R15) to the drug trafficker
(friend of the judge)
              armed to the teeth?

Manan lejos a oscuras

Espejean bajo tierra
al tacto al ojo esquivas
aguas
          que labran
manantiales, atraviesan la piedra.

Aguas dolientes
mudas de un Eldorado
líquido que de agua dulce
irriga basaltos litosfera
secretas venas
cármenes
acechados por la sed de inversores / bonistas

Acuífero que baña
el sol prieto del suelo vertientes
de ora azul. Napas a ciegas
Limpias aguas secretas del solar guaraní:
                    que tu riqueza mane
                    nos alcance
                    tu maná no amenace.

              amén.

Flowing Far into the Dark

Waters gleam underground
to the touch to the eye elusive
waters
           that feed
springs, cross rock

Mournful mute
waters of a liquid
El Dorado that with sweet fresh water
irrigates the basalt mantel
secret crimson
veins
watched by thirsty investors / bondholders

Aquifer that bathes
the sun the dark earthen slopes
with blue gold. Blind subterranean mantel
Clean secret waters of the Guarani ancestral home:
           that your wealth flows
           that our reach
           does not threaten your manna.

           amen.

el habla desangrada anegó la cuidad
dejó sin casa sin oficio inundados
los ojos del relato

el ser y el cuerpo en territorio ajeno en paso de frontera
en paso falso

barrenado la voz / borroso el nombre
(no la marca commercial del champión)

desvalijado el yo

    apenas
    la poesía puede tantear a ciegas
    rastrear a pie descalzo
    en el puro dolor
    mudo en su ancha mancha
    urbana / círculo de condenados

            por cometer pecado
    de indigencia pecado
    original: haber nacido

    de madre y padre
    pobres. linaje
    de excluidos.

the bloodless speech drowns the city
leaves the flooded without homes, without jobs
the eyes of the story

being and body on foreign territory at foreign border crossing
a wrong move

the voice drilling / the name blurred
(not the brand name of an athletic shoe)

robbed of self

      poetry can barely
      feel the way blindly
      to track on foot barefoot
      in the pure pain
      mute in its broad urban
      blight / circle of condemned

          for committing the sin
      of indigence, the original
      sin: having been born

      to a poor mother
      father: lineage
      of the excluded.

circe maia

y teresa andruetto—otoño 2012—conversan
               para vientodefondo

hojeo en el bus—setiembre 2013— / en casa tomo
               la pesadora de perlas

gramaje del papel es piel de fruta, se desliza la mano
La descubre

cada línea del diálogo despierta enlaza ojos y páginas

la magia de una foto aún captura/
               erguida
en un gesto que el mirar acompaña
una mano de circe señala el fondo (parral en hora
de vendimia solar): follaje claroscuro, muro, espejados
unen/separan
la mesa de la casa donde ellas charlan, tapizada de libros
y el trasvidrio
desde donde la cámara
dispara/captala luz del otro lado (la ventana del frente
transparenta follajes de la calle): el interior transido
de palabras e imágenes en viaje
adentro/afuera. tras la fotografía
               de gastón sironi, en páginas siguientes

flamea el peso leve
de las perlas
que pesan en su luz interior en su lengua común
las dos mujeres

Circe Maia

and Teresa Andruetto—-fall 2012—interview
                    for Viento de Fondo Press

I leaf through it on the bus—September 2013— / at home again pick up
                    la pesadora de perlas. the weigher of pearls

the weight of paper fruit skin, the hand slides
discovers

each line of dialogue awakes connects eyes and page

the magic of a photo even captures /
                    upright
in a gesture the glance follows
Circe's hand waving toward the garden (grape arbor in time
of harvest sun): foliage chiaroscuro, wall, mirror-like
uniting/ separating
the table of the house where they chat, upholstered in books
and the window
through which the camera
shoots/captures the light of the other side (the front window reflecting
foliage of the street): the interior full
of words and images traveling
inside/out. after the photograph
                    by gaston sironi, in the following pages

flames the slight blush
of the pearls
that the two women weigh in their inner light
in their common language

como una fruta seca. así es la joya. almendra
nuez. abiertas sus dos valvas de plata. gemelas. cóncavas.
llevan ligados labios
las dos alas del cofre. son dos naves
hermanas. genitales. que guardan
un tesoro / vidrio embrionario / saco de cristal breve.
la silueta de un ave de titanio / fisonomía fósil en la matriz
del huevo / prendido a la placenta transparente.

cerrará sus postigos sus celosías la joya. un párpado
de plata emplumará progenie y pulimento / brillo de luna
en cuencos que al cerrarse cobijarán
oficio de tijeras de martillo y estrellas. guardada
como en fruto de mar
en la ley del oficio en sus reglas
de amor y torbellino y miedo

el temblor de la plata escudará
el secreto. vivirá

              el broche

prendido a fugaces fulgores a prendas que soporte
darán
y engarce
al sueño / madreperla / de unas manos de orfebre
ceñidas a su sed de maternal
episodios de luz

en vestidos y cuerpos.

(por el broche de lilián lipchitz)

106

like a dried fruit. it's like that, the jewel. an almond.
the two silver valves open. identical twins. concave.
their lips bound
the two wings of a chest. they are two ships.
sisters. genitals. that guard
a treasure / embryonic glass / brief crystal jacket.
the silhouette of a titanium bird / fossil physiognomy in the matrix
of the egg / lit by the transparent placenta

the jewel will close its shutters its latticework. a silver eyelid
will adorn with feathered progeny and polish / brightness of the moon
in hollows that, having closed, will shelter
the trade of scissors made from hammer and stars, guarded
like fruit of the sea
in the law of the trade in its rules
of love and maelstrom and fear

the tremor of the silver will hide
the secret. it will live

                    the broach

caught on the fleeting brilliance of garments that give
their support
setting
for the dream / mother of pearl / of some goldsmith's hands
clinging to their thirst for maternal
moments of light

on dresses and bodies.

(after a broach by lilián lipchitz)

107

Óvulo del deseo

El verdadero deseo empieza así: después. Al otro día.

El día después, a solas con el propio cuerpo y cuando ya no hay nada que pensar ni que decidir, lo que empieza a existir es el deseo del deseo.

Un embrión que crece como si hubiera sido fecundado por el trámite torpe del anterior y su fracaso.

Como si el deseo hubiera estado ovulando. Como si solo aceptara ser despertado de a poco. Con la dignidad lenta, aristocrática, de lo que estuvo siempre.

Ovum of desire

The real desire starts like this: later. The next day.

The day after, alone with your own body and when there is nothing to think or decide, what begins to exist is the desire for desire.

An embryo that grows as if it had been fertilized by the previous clumsy procedure and its failure.

As if the desire had been ovulating. As if it only agreed to be awakened little by little. With the slow dignity, aristocratic, of what always was.

"Sea la niebla aliada y no enemiga."

—Ida Vitale

Neblina
así la nombran
La enfermedad del siglo 21 en su fe de bautismo dice llamarse así:
Neblina
El nombre aroma húmedo huele a parque acaricia
tiende un velo de gotas que iridesce que brilla
suele nublar el banco de hormigón
la valla los portales
levar la señalética del barrio en sus brazos traslúcidos amparar
transeúntes en su capa de chispas
y entornando los ojos envolver
los follajes

La neblina es así, esa sí es la neblina

Marea de rocío banco de aguas milésimas
que agrupa y desdibuja, extravía y conecta
las piezas del paisaje

Tras su amnios de luz emulsionada tras su tul fenoménico
también traga o repara
las piezas de la vida

la Neblina mental, así llamada.

"May the fog be an ally and not the enemy."

—Ida Vitale

Fog
they named it
On the baptismal certificate of this 21st century disease it reads, my name is:
                                                                    Fog
The name caresses damp aroma a scent of park
stretches a veil of drops that iridesce that shine
clouds the concrete bench
the fence the doorways
raises the neighborhood signs in its translucent arms to protect
passers-by in its sparkling cloak
and half-closes their eyes to shroud
them in greenery.

The fog is like that, yes, that is fog

Tide of dew reservoir of water thousands of thousandths
gather and blur, misplace and connect
pieces of the landscape

behind its amniotic membrane of milky light behind its tactile tulle
                it also swallows or repairs
                the pieces of life

Fog, it is called. Mental fog.

Jardines

Imaginá un jardín. Capaz que no sos capaz de imaginar porque mientras tratás de inventar imágenes se interponen las de otros que conociste en la infancia o en un viaje y no te dejan imaginar. Capaz que un paquete de paisajes clásicos—jardines versallescos, jardines de la Alhambra, jardines acuáticos de Monet en Giverny—empieza a descargarse a ritmo de postales programadas y hasta te complica la intención de evocar por lo menos aquellos otros que viste laborados a mano. A ver si te empeñás en volver a fijar la atención por lo menos en éstos, asomados al frente de sus casas con gesto de coquetería o instilados de humor meláncolico o, si no, por lo menos algo de ellos aunque no puedas imaginarte otros que nunca viste. A ver si ves la rama de jazmín, el macizo nocturno cargado de botones y mirando para adentro bien adentro volvés a ver cómo se sentía el relente perfumado de las flores invisibles.

Si ya hiciste la tentativa vas despejando el camino. Ahora vas a tratar de imaginar otros jardines, otros que nunca viste ni en foto.

Otros. Enclavados en una isla. Pero antes de ir a esos otros necesitarías saber si mantener un jardín—un jardín familiar laborado a mano con la espalda y las rodillas dobladas—puede considerarse lujo o debe considerarse necesidad. El rango antropológico del jardín quisieras conocer, alguien lo debe de haber estudiado. La razón de ser de un predio de tierra recortada en parcelas pequeñas al lado de la vivienda, al frente o al fondo, donde se cultivan flores y algún árbol que también florecerá. Eso es lo que quisieras saber. (No te vas a estar preguntando por desmedidos jardines palaciegos, claro, ni por groserías a lo Dubai. Igual te gustaría por curiosidad saber algo sobre los Jardines Colgantes—los cuales al parecer no colgaban sino que asomaban palmeras y datileros en Babilonia—o según otras versiones en Nínive, Mosul hoy, es decir: tierra arrasada hoy.)

Por la razón de ser de los jardines familiares te preguntás. Necesitás conocer la ontología del vínculo entre el jardín y quienes lo plantan mientras lo van imaginando crecer y lo mantienen vivo.

Mirado de esta forma es un vínculo de reciprocidad. El jardín da trabajo pero también da alegría y quien enjardina da vida (alegría de vivir al fin de

Gardens

Imagine a garden. Perhaps you're not able to imagine one because while you try to invent images, ones you knew in childhood or on a trip interpose themselves and do not let you imagine. Perhaps a package of classic landscapes—Versailles gardens, gardens of the Alhambra, the aquatic gardens of Monet in Giverny—begins to download to the rhythm of programmed postcards and it complicates your intention to evoke at least those you saw worked by hand. At least, see if you can give your attention to these, peeking out from in front of their houses with a coquettish expression or instilled with melancholy humor or, if not, at least imagine some of them, even if you can not imagine other gardens you've never seen. See if you can imagine the branch of jasmine, the night mountains full of buttercups. And looking inside way inside, you can see again how the fragrant dew of invisible flowers felt.

If already you have made the attempt you are clearing the way. Now you can try to imagine other gardens, others you never saw in any photo.

Others. Nestled on an island. But before going to those others, you would need to know if maintaining a garden—a family garden worked by hand with the back and knees bent—can be considered a luxury or should be considered a necessity. What is anthropological range of the garden you would like to come to know. Someone must have studied it. The raison d'etre of land cut into small plots next to the house, in front or at the back, where flowers are grown and a tree that will also bloom. That is what you would like to know. (You will not be asking for excessive palace gardens, of course, nor for rude follies like those of Dubai.) You would like to know something about the Hanging Gardens—which apparently did not hang, but rather had palm trees and date palms peeking out on Babylon—-as the versions still do in Nineveh, Mosul, meaning: scorched earth today.)

For what reason do family gardens exist you ask yourself. You need to know the ontology of the link between the garden and those who plant it while imagining that will grow and that they will be able keep it alive.

Looked at in this way there is a bond of reciprocity. The garden takes work but also gives joy and those who garden give life (joy of living at the

cuentas) a klivias, amarilis, damas de la noche y se toma trabajo, se lo asigna encorvado o de rodillas. Es importante saber eso, qué es lo que tienen sostienen entre sí jardines y personas, para poder imaginarse la desaparición del jardín. Porque el jardín desaparecerá antes o después de que desaparezcan las manos que lo atienden.

Ahora tenés que imaginar jardines. Los que nunca viste. Los de una isla. Entera. Tenés que verlos desaparecer a todos antes que a ellas. En los hoyos abiertos por el rastrillaje verás algunos restos minúsculos, raicillas entreveradas al grano arcilloso de los surcos, mullidos por el pico y la pala. Todo ha ocurrido tan bruscamente que no has tenido tiempo de imaginar la elegancia de los tallos ni la redondez de los capullos ni el color de los pétalos ni la sombra de las hojas del árbol en el mediodía de primavera. Todo ha ocurrido así porque las jerarquías del orden mundial han paralizado el tránsito de las abejas en torno a estambres pistilos corolas desterrando el futuro de tulipanes gladiolos azucenas jacintos lirios fresias cuyos bulbos desentierran las manos ocupadas en salvar la vida, en salvarse del hambre. Imaginás miles de espaldas dobladas hacia las camas de cultivo de hortalizas y granos, miles de manos rascando la tierra, desdoblándola, sacudiéndola como se sacuden las sábanas, aireando el lecho vacío, sacudiéndose la maldición del bloqueo. Miles de uñas desveladas en la tarea de horadarlo con semillas y plantines, en la causa revolucionaria de dar vuelta tierra, en la conjura de almácigos y surcos abiertos, en el levantamiento de cañas y estacas tutoras de pimientos habas pepinos tomates, en la revuelta de los jardineros, en los prosélitos de la papaya y el apio de espaldas al cielo. De espaldas al cielo de la isla asediada. De espaldas al cerco económico. Inclinados a la tierra. De hinojos en ella.

114

end of the day) to Kaffir lilies, amaryllis, Queen of the Night cactus and it takes work, assigning yourself bending or kneeling. It is important to know this, what claim gardens and people have on each other to able to imagine the disappearance of the garden. Because the garden will disappear before or after the hands that serve it disappear.

Now you have to imagine gardens. The ones you never saw. Those on an island. Whole. You have to see them disappear, totally, before they do. In the holes opened by raking you will see some tiny remains, rootlets interspersed with the clay grain of the furrows, loosened by beak and shovel. Everything has happened so abruptly that you've not had time to imagine the elegance of the stems or the roundness of the buds or the color of the petals or the shade of the tree leaves in the midday of spring. All this has happened this way because the hierarchies of the world order have paralyzed the traffic of bees around stamens pistils corollas banishing the future of tulips gladiolus lilies hyacinths irises freesias whose bulbs the workers dig up to save their lives, save themselves from hunger. Imagine thousands of backs bent over the beds of vegetables and of grain, thousands of hands scratching the earth, unfolding it, shaking it as sheets are shaken, airing the empty bed, shaking off the curse of the blockade. Thousands of fingernails kept awake by the task of piercing the earth for seeds and seedlings, in the revolutionary cause of returning to the land, in a plot, a conspiracy, of transplanting and open furrows, of raising canes and stakes for peppers beans cucumbers tomatoes, in the revolt of the gardeners, in the proselytes of papaya and celery with their backs to the sky. With their backs to the sky of the besieged island. With their back to the economic siege. Inclined to the earth. Planting fennel.

Por qué

ha de enajenarse la poesía
a la estética ajena: la de show.

Si ella es fundación
en el desasimiento

si ella es desazón

casa en el agua.

Why

has poetry gone mad
for the aesthetics of others: for a show.

      If poetry is the foundation
      of detachment

      if it's disquiet

      the house in the water.

Naturaleza muerta con derrotas

Hay que saber perder
y al acercase
tocar

con la mano seguro la medusa

tocar como a una fruta
la curva del dolor

la floral taciturna medida
del fracaso

en la cesta grupal de panes y derrotas
donde
caben
la mano las uvas las almendras.

Still Life with Defeats

You must know how to lose
and draw near
to touch

the jellyfish with a sure hand

to touch like a fruit
the curve of pain

the mute floral measure
of failure

in the collective basket of bread and defeats
where there is
room
for the hand the grapes the almonds.

The Author

Tatiana Oroño (San José, Uruguay, 1947) is Uruguayan poet, writer and teacher. She is the author of nine books including *Libro de horas* (2017), *Estuario* (2015) and *La Piedra Nada Sabe* (2008). *Still Life with Defeats: Selected Poems of Tatiana Oroño* is the first English-language collection of Oroño's poetry. In 2009, Oroño won the Bartolomé Hidalgo Prize in Poetry and the Morosoli Prize for Poetry, two of the most important Uruguayan literary prizes. Her poems have been published in Argentina, Bolivia, Brazil, Canada, Cuba, Chile, El Salvador, Spain, France, and Mexico and, translated by Jesse Lee Kercheval, in literary magazines such as *American Poetry Review, Guernica, Ploughshares, Stand, Western Humanities Review*, and *World Literature Today*.

The Translator

Jesse Lee Kercheval is a poet, fiction writer, memoirist and translator, specializing in Uruguayan poetry. Her books include *America that island off the coast of France*, winner of the Dorset Prize, *The Alice Stories*, winner of the Prairie Schooner Fiction Book Prize; and the memoir *Space*, winner of the Alex Award from the American Library Association. Her translations include *The Invisible Bridge: Selected Poems of Circe Maia, Fable of an Inconsolable Man* by Javier Etchevarren, *Reborn in Ink* by Laura Cesarco Eglin, co-translated with Catherine Jagoe, and *Night in the North* by Fabian Severo, co-translated with Laura Cesarco Eglin. She is currently the Zona Gale Professor of English at the University of Wisconsin-Madison.